Original Colorblind
Fine Art Photography

Decades of being around accomplished artists producing absolutely phenomenal quality work has taught that we are capable of greatness. It is possible to meet our destiny and become it. Experiencing excellence done with such apparent magical ease and humble selfless gratification is the inspiration for this original photography. It is an expression of freedom.

Being colorblind gives an advantage when composing black & white... less confusion. This collection selected from thousands of captures. All images were framed in the camera and presented without edits, genuine as seen through the lens. RAW conversion applied by proprietary panchromatic process.

Fine art prints available from original files.

info@ BeachNoise.com

Joseph Fleming

0125

0354

0437

0503

0531

0705

0780

0826

0920

0938

1085

1088

1581

1608

1784

1976

2068

2180

2397

2467

2495

2631

2929

3147

3151

3359

3714

3720

3799

3916

3943

4035

4070

4099

4193

4265

4533

4560

4879

5492

5541

5750

5784

5811

5844

5846

6095

6176

6946

7148

7182

7339

7656

7693

7783

7939

8173

8345

8470

8471

8766

8889

9024

9297

9353

9430

9970

9975

9980

9992

www.ingramcontent.com/pod-product-compliance
Lightning Source LLC
Chambersburg PA
CBHW040838180526
45159CB00001B/228